A bridge too far: the phobic reaction

Suppose you are crossing Hungerford Bridge in London with someone who suffers from Gephyrophobia – a fear of crossing bridges. As you walk from Embankment underground station and ascend the stone steps which take you onto the bridge, your companion starts to talk nervously about the prospect of crossing it. You arrive on the bridge and his body begins to stiffen, his head held very still as he stares straight ahead. After a few steps he begins to sweat and holds on to your hand, clutching it tighter and tighter as you guide him across. You notice that he cannot help glancing downwards into the water, especially through the gap between the pedestrian bridge and the railway bridge to which it is attached. Unmistakable signs of panic are taking him over as you arrive at the centre of your crossing – profuse sweating, rapid breathing and heartbeat, clenched muscles and a wide-eyed look of fear. You try to say something to calm him down. 'Don't talk!', he says. All of his concentration is being mustered to take on the task in hand. Suddenly he exhales deeply and his body relaxes. He releases his grip on your hand and starts to walk more confidently forward. 'What's happened?', you ask. 'It's okay once I've got halfway over', he says, and you are left pondering the origin and development of such a phobia.

Helter skelter: science of the irrational

Most people do not question why a child is scared of the dark, or why a person hates tomatoes. We slide the emotional response and the putative stimulus together. 'I hate tomatoes.' In the simple declarative we posit a causal relation between the psychological output 'hate' and the culinary input 'tomatoes'. If someone comes along and asks 'Why?', we feel uncomfortable, not wanting our likes and dislikes to be scrutinised too closely. Freud realised that the supposed chain of causality was little more than an illusion. Inputs and outputs did not really 'add up'. By questioning the equation between 'stimulus' and 'response' he announced the influence of unconscious factors in the mind.

Ernest Jones, Freud's disciple and biographer, listed three senses in which things did not add up in the physiology and psychology of anxiety reactions:

1. A 'disproportion between the external stimulus and the response'.
2. A 'disharmony between bodily and mental manifestations'.
3. An 'internal disharmony' within the body or mind itself.

The first of these is the most obvious. We find it in some of our greatest literary creations. Scholars have spent endless hours debating the reasons for Hamlet's excessive overreaction to, and preoccupation with, his father's death. Doesn't he realise that fathers die all the time? Hamlet's reaction is quite out of proportion to the stated facts as they are presented, and this, says T.S. Eliot, is the reason why *Hamlet* is not a great work of art. It doesn't add up. It's out of proportion. There is no 'objective correlative' that makes it make sense.[1] But what is a failure of art for Eliot is proof of the unconscious for Freud. The lack of proportion between the experiential input and the excessive reactive output is precisely what indicates the influence of another level of meaning and determination, both in the text and in the reader.

And the same is true of phobias. In stating the obvious – that crossing a bridge is not a death-defying endeavour – psychoanalysis justifies its concept of the unconscious and its mode of inquiry through free association. If it frightens you to death nevertheless, there must be something else going on.

But what if the danger were real? Suppose the bullets were flying, the bombs were dropping and the hand grenades exploding all around you? Writing between the wars, Ernest Jones was not very sympathetic. 'How much distress, for instance', he inquires,

should be allotted as normal for someone exposed to an air raid during the war, or still more for someone exposed to the appalling conditions of the actual front, without recourse being had to patho-logical factors?

Warming to his theme, he continues:

Generosity is prone in such cases to make con-siderable allowances for the situation and to pass over responses of anxiety as natural and inevitable which perhaps a more critical mood would scrutinise more strictly.[2]

This might seem insensitive; it also points to a change of focus. Little more than a decade later, Anna Freud opened her residential nurseries for children who had been bombed out in the Blitz. She discovered that it was not the bombs and destruction of their homes that was traumatic for the children, but the separation from – and worries about – their parents.[3]

The second point is less easy to notice. There is something out of kilter between the mind and the body. They don't seem to be reading the same script. A politician may give a brilliantly controlled speech at his party conference, yet find himself drenched in sweat or suffering palpitations. In his mind there is no fear. Only in his body does fear ooze out from every pore. Or let's say you take a child to a theme park. She is anticipating a 'scary' ride that she has heard about or seen before. It's really scary. You realise that her excited talk is not relieving the tension, it is turning the screw of her anxious expectation. She is winding herself up. The signs of fear build to a crescendo while waiting in the inevitable queue. She doesn't want to go on the ride, she wants to go home. She is too scared. Taking the Ernest Jones approach, you say: 'Don't be pathetic – pull yourself together, you little twerp', and clip her round the ear. Once you have dragged her onto the ride – you're not going to waste nearly an hour waiting for nothing – you realise that far from being consumed with fear, her screams and bodily reactions correspond to excitement and pleasure. 'Can we go again?', she says, as you disembark.

In a companion volume to this one, Graham Music recounts an experiment in which mothers leave their toddlers suddenly in a room. Some children cry and get upset, others seem hardly to notice the departure or return of their mothers.

Yet, when the pulse rate, adrenalin and cortisol levels of both groups are measured, we see that all have similar physiological reactions to their mothers' disappearance.[4]

The third disharmony identified by Jones is a kind of fragmentation of mental faculties. He calls it an 'inco-ordination' in the mind itself, and notices that when you are really frightened there is a curious mixture of over-excitation with paralysis. My friend walking across the bridge neither plays dead nor runs away. His body is at once stiff and unresponsive, yet agitated. He feels nauseous. His head is spinning. He is not ready for action, he is just ready to implode. He is frightened of something, yet his attention is not directed to any particular source of danger. He finds himself in a strange mental state that makes no sense as far as biological survival is concerned. It doesn't add up in the ledger of natural selection.

The phobic reaction contains elements of all the incompatibilities, disharmonies and inconsistencies that Jones describes. A phobia does not 'make sense'. It is an *irrational* fear. And that is the defining feature that opens it up to a science of the irrational – psychoanalysis.

Charles and Alfred: theories of phobia

It is not easy to say why, in a particular situation, a phobia is produced rather than an inhibition, or a somatic symptom, or a diffuse state of anxiety. Psychical events have many causes – 'overdetermined', Freud calls it. For any developmental outcome there is a complex play of forces clamouring to be expressed, and it is impossible to predict how the dice will eventually fall. Nevertheless, phobias and phobic phenomena are typical during certain periods of childhood, and adult phobias can often be traced back to earlier forms which preceded them. There are two common non-psychoanalytic theories of phobias which have achieved the status of 'common sense'. The first is a biological theory which assumes that phobias – such as the fear of spiders or snakes or high places – are leftovers from our evolutionary past and refer to real dangers faced by our ancestors.

Most of us have a sense of repulsion if we meet with a snake. Snake phobia, we might say, is a universal human characteristic; and Darwin has described most impressively how he could not avoid feeling fear of a snake that struck at him, even though he was protected by a thick sheet of glass.[5]

Freud's sympathy with the argument should not blind us to the fact that jumping away from a striking snake is not the equivalent of a snake phobia. Genetic explanations are also limited in scope, unable to explain the multitude of phobias that actually exist. Further, since we succeed in passing on our genes if we respond to danger in an appropriate way, it is difficult to see how the genetic argument can account for the curious incapacity that overwhelms the person with a phobia when faced with the object of their fear.

The second non-psychoanalytic view is a simple 'trauma' theory, which has achieved the ultimate credibility of being the basis of a BBC television series.[6] A child is afraid of dogs because, when he was little, a dog jumped up to his push-chair and frightened him. Another is worried that Red Indians will attack her at home after she saw the film *Calamity Jane*. The phobia is a conditioned response to traumatic experience. In the post-Freudian films of Alfred Hitchcock, numerous characters exhibit phobias. The trauma theory is enlisted to explain their motivation or to effect narrative resolution. Thus the eponymous heroine of *Marnie* has a murderous childhood secret expressed in her fear of lightning and the colour red; the policeman who let his partner drop and suffers ever after from a fear of heights, falls for the wrong girl in *Vertigo*; the psychiatrist without a past unaccountably fears the white of a tablecloth in *Spellbound*. When Hitchcock himself was asked if he had ever been really frightened about anything, he would simply reply: 'Always.'[7] On other occasions he would tell a story from his childhood. He was always terrified of being alone, but at six years old, after committing some domestic misdemeanour, his stern father sent him to the police station with a note. The duty officer dutifully read the note and locked young Alfred in a cell for some minutes. He was scared of policemen after that, but the experience taught him an important lesson in life: don't get arrested.

The Birds: representing the inner world

The trauma idea seems a plausible explanation until it is discovered that, for instance, the phobia only develops some years after the alleged traumatic incident, or that the incident itself is only known through information given by parents. Tracing the phobia back to the traumatic scenario, we often find a more complex synthesis of factors. In one example, a paralysing fear of birds and feathers was linked to the moment when a bird flew into a room and could not get out. A child was with her grandmother, unable to cope as the terrified bird flew around the room bumping into things and shedding feathers across the floor. The child, too, became terrified, observing the frantic efforts of the bird to escape and her grandmother's flustered attempts to help it.[8] Psychoanalysts would unpack the elements of this story and give due weight to each: the factor of helplessness, the absence of the mother, the grandmother's fear, the loss of parts of the bird's body, the fear of attack, the sense of being trapped, the bird as embodiment of aggression, the association of birds (in some cultures and folklore) with death, and so on. The traumatic incident is not seen as an aberrant intrusion into the calm waters of a happy childhood, but as part of the wider story of the person's emotional life, with its inevitable storms and dangerous currents of feeling.

Birds fly around the room in Hitchcock's masterpiece, *The Birds*, based on a story by Daphne du Maurier.[9] It is a drama in which the principal male character is relegated to the margins of the narrative. Although the (dead) father is significant, it is relationships between women that pivot the story around the ineffectual lawyer 'Mitch' Brenner. If 'Hitch' himself was scared of policemen and the law, it was his mother and her surrogates who dominated his life. 'Even after his marriage, his mother often went along on vacation with him and his wife, and on those occasions he was more concerned with her than with his wife.'[10]

In the story, a younger woman and an older woman – a mother – struggle over possession of the son. When socialite Melanie Daniels follows Mitch to his home town of Bodega Bay with a gift of lovebirds for his younger sister Cathy, she brings with her a plague of biblical proportions. The aggressively attacking birds testify to something within the emotional dynamics of the story. Most often this is interpreted as the mother's aggression unleashed in response to a threat that the sexually expressive Melanie represents. However, with all due respect to Oedipus, this is not a simple Oedipal drama. Struggles within the dyadic relationship between mother and daughter take centre stage, as well as the mother's vulnerability and fear of abandonment.

In the following scene, Melanie and Annie, the local teacher and an ex-girlfriend of Mitch, are discussing his mother Lydia:

Annie: *You know, her attitude nearly drove me crazy. I simply couldn't understand it. When I got back to San Francisco I spent days trying to figure out just what I'd done to displease her.*

Melanie: *And what had you done?*

Annie: *Nothing! I simply existed. So what was the answer? A jealous woman, right? A clinging possessive mother.* (She shakes her head.) *Wrong. With all due respect to Oedipus, I don't think that was the case at all.*

Melanie: *Then what was it?*

Annie: *Lydia liked me you see. That was the strange part of it. In fact, now that I am no longer a threat, we're very good friends.*

Melanie: *Then why did she object to you?*

Annie: *Because she was afraid.*

Melanie: *Afraid you'd take Mitch? ...*

Annie: *No, I don't think so. She's not afraid of losing her son, you see. She's only afraid of being abandoned.*

But it's not hard to see the consequences of defiance of the mother. Later in the same scene, Melanie asks Annie if she should go to Cathy's party.

Melanie: *Do you think I should go?*

Annie: *That's up to you.*

Melanie: *It's really up to Lydia, isn't it?*

Annie: *Never mind Lydia. Do you want to go?*

Melanie (firmly): *Yes.*

Annie: *Then go.*

The room is silent. Melanie nods, slowly, and then smiles. [...]

Suddenly into the silence, comes a THUMP

outside, startling them both. The thump is made by a seagull that has smashed itself into the door.

The four central female figures form a complex network of attachments – Melanie, Lydia, Annie and Cathy. Each of them could be responsible for the birds. There is rage against mothers (from Melanie), against daughters (from Lydia) or siblings (from Annie), and fear of abandonment in all of them. In the birds, there are more than birds: they represent a dimension of unconscious female experience. They demonstrate the underlying conflict in the mother–daughter bond, and potential dangers to negotiate in the process of growing up. Similar themes are found in *Snow White*, *Cinderella* and many other mythic confrontations between mothers and daughters.

Psychoanalytic explanations of phobia are thus concerned with the inner world. In particular they assign a determining influence to 'phantasy', 'anxiety' and 'psychic conflict', especially the conflict between love and aggression (ambivalence). A woman with a 'worm phobia' did not report any traumatic experience. But she did report a tormenting phantasy from her sixth year – that she was buried alive and exposed to worms.

The lion, the witch and the wardrobe: imaginary dangers

The description of my friend crossing Hungerford Bridge clearly shows a phobia in its capacity as an 'irrational fear'. The phobic person does not really know why he is afraid, any more than a person who laughs at a joke knows why he is laughing. It seems silly to say: 'I am afraid of crossing bridges.' Recognition of the 'irrationality', however, makes little difference to its psychical reality for the phobic person. In the grip of the phobic reaction, the phobic individual exists in a peculiar state of knowing something and not knowing it at the same time. The phobic object exists in two mental registers at once, both equally real to the person. Discussing the common phobias of childhood, Anna Freud recounts the story of a little girl with a fear of lions:

This child countered the well-meant assurances of her father that lions could not climb up to her bedroom by saying plaintively that, of course, her father talked of real lions who could not climb, but her own lions were more than capable . . .[11]

In phobias, as with all neuroses, we move in 'the no-man's land between reality and fantasy'.[12] The child believes avidly in the reality of the phobic symbol, despite the strength of his intellectual assessment. Children, too, can be stupid. Such premature debility of the child's intellect led Freud to assume that a phobia was not a simple fear of an external object or situation which could be escaped through avoidance, but a response to a threat located within the mind. A child who avoids school because of bullying is in a different situation from one who avoids school because some inchoate panic overwhelms him at the school gates. He just hates school. Both are 'school-phobic' in the descriptive sense – they both avoid school – but only the latter is school-phobic in what Freud calls the 'dynamic' sense, in which the fear is fuelled from within. In the case of the school-phobic child, we might find an intolerable fear that the mother will disappear or die when he leaves her. Hard and fast distinctions are difficult to make in practice, but from a theoretical point of view it is useful to regard phobias as responses to the demands of the inner world.

Having taken this step from the outer world to the inner, we are no longer surprised to find inconsistencies in the matter of knowing and not knowing, or questions of belief. Dreams are a nightly reminder that we can believe in almost anything. Have you ever, while dreaming, said to yourself, 'It's only a dream'? Or woken yourself up and started again? We know we are dreaming when we are dreaming, yet inside the dream its contents carry conviction. We know and do not know at the same time. We believe in a world populated by objects and experiences that have not, will not and cannot happen in reality. Philosophers discuss the truth conditions attached to the King of France's beard (there is no King of France), but in our dream we may be more concerned with the pea soup that he has inadvertently spilled down it.

If our mind harbours kings and princes that do not exist, it also harbours demons and goblins. In the dreams of children we see fears embodied, given private form in a manner that resonates with the more public representations of myth and fairy tale. Consider these dreams of a normal seven-year-old girl:

Dream 1

I was in a room in the dark; it was pitch black, but I could still see. The room was guarded by monsters and I escaped with other people (I was the leader), but all the other people got caught. I ran into an alley, there were lots of doors and monsters all around. In the alley was an old witch. In my head I heard the words, 'No one who goes down this alley ever comes out . . . Ha, ha, ha . . .', then I saw a flash of light that lighted up the old witch's face that was really frightening.

Dream 2

I went through a door. It was an old house that

looked like a museum. When I went in, everything was yellow and there were men in yellow suits swinging on trapezes and they were laughing (in a malevolent way). On the floor there were all these spiders and there were dips in the floor that the spiders were crawling about in. I kept running but I tripped over and landed to see a really big spider – like the queen spider – right by my face, and I screamed.

Dream 3

I was being chased by something and I came to a cliff. I thought I was going to fall off it, but I jumped off and flew away. I flew for hours. It was really fun and a really good dream.

We are not surprised to hear of dreams populated by witches and spiders and devouring monsters. Few of us are so detached from our childhood selves that this strikes us as an alien experience. Psychoanalysts would see in the witch figure a representation of the mother – the 'bad mother' as we created her in phantasy.[13] Just as the goddesses of antiquity were both deities of creation and destruction,[14] so the mother may be an object of both love and fear. Mothers change all the time. We would like to imagine that nothing could be more stable than the figure of the mother on whom we base our sense of security. Yet they frustrate us and torment us as well as relieve and protect us. Children love them, fear them and fear *for* them.

In Donald Winnicott's famous case of 'The Piggle', the frightening figures of the dream world spill over into the waking world of a two-and-a-half-year-old girl. After her mother's confinement and the birth of her sister Susan, Gabrielle's personality began to change, displaying considerable anxiety and a lack of freedom in her play. She called to her parents till late at night, tormented by elaborate fantasies, unable to go to sleep. 'She has a black mummy and daddy', explained her parents:

The black mummy comes in after her at night and says: 'Where are my yams?' . . . Sometimes she is put into the toilet by the black mummy. The black mummy, who lives in her tummy, and who can be talked to on the telephone, is often ill and difficult to make better.[15]

In a subsequent letter, her father said: 'Going to bed created a major scene – as happens quite often now. She says she is frightened of the black mummy coming after her.'[16] But if the 'black mummy' only exists in the realm of the imagination, if it only has reality from the inside, then the question arises: of what is she really frightened? 'She seems to be suffering greatly from what was once called "a sense of sin"', wrote her father.[17]

The naked diner: psychical mechanisms for phobia formation

It should not have taken so long to establish the obvious: that it is not the phobic object which is really frightening; and that the source of fear is inside the mind. Such a conclusion could have been predicted on logical grounds alone when one considers the multiplicity of phobias. Here is a selected list:

Allodoxaphobia – fear of opinions.

Anemophobia – fear of air drafts or wind.

Ataxophobia – fear of disorder or untidiness.

Automatonophobia – fear of ventriloquists' dummies, animatronic creatures, wax statues: anything that falsely represents a sentient being.

Bufonophobia – fear of toads.

Ergophobia – fear of work.

Eurotophobia – fear of female genitalia.

Gephyrophobia, Gephydrophobia, or Gephysrophobia – fear of crossing bridges.

Hellenologophobia – fear of Greek terms or complex scientific terminology.

Mastigophobia – fear of punishment.

Misophobia – fear of being contaminated with dirt or germs. (Also Verminophobia – fear of germs.)

Neophobia – fear of anything new.

Nyctophobia – fear of the dark or of night.

Octophobia – fear of the figure 8.

Ophthalmophobia – fear of being stared at.

Oneirophobia – fear of dreams.

Ornithophobia – fear of birds.

Papyrophobia – fear of paper.

Paraphobia – fear of sexual perversion.

Phobophobia – fear of phobias.

Phonophobia – fear of noises or voices or one's own voice.

Scatophobia – fear of faecal matter.

Scelerophobia – fear of bad men, burglars.

Siderodromophobia – fear of trains, railways or train travel.

Social Phobia – fear of being evaluated negatively in social situations.

Sociophobia – fear of society or people in general.

Telephonophobia – fear of telephones.

Thanatophobia or Thantophobia – fear of death or dying.

Xenophobia – fear of strangers or foreigners.

Zoophobia – fear of animals.

At least we can be sure that Stanley Hall, who devised this nomenclature, did not suffer from Hellenologophobia. 'It sounds like a list of the ten plagues of Egypt', Freud remarked drily, 'though their number goes far beyond ten'.[18] But how is the phobic object imbued with the qualities which cause panic or anxiety? Where do these qualities come from, and how do they then rebound on the phobic person?

Consider the last of the three dreams above. The optimistic and grandiose transcendence of fear in the dream fails to obscure the ultimate indeterminacy of the danger: 'I was being chased by . . . something.' This nebulous apprehension transforms into a specific object: 'I came to a cliff.' And in defining the fear – objectifying it – the subject finds a means of escape: 'I jumped off and flew away.' The narrative of the dream mirrors the psychological process by which a phobia might be created. Unnameable fears within the mind are externalised and given form.

But what is the source of fear? What lurks inside, threatening, ever ready to attack? How can it be that part of our selves should be traitor to ourselves? It took no genius to see that human passions may undermine the integrity of our rational self. Poets, artists and philosophers before

Freud told of the horrors and dangers that human passions could provoke. Our emotional lives, forged in a cauldron of dependency which is our biological fate, must be moderated and controlled if they are not to torment us with their demands. In *The Interpretation of Dreams*, Freud says the following about dreams of wild animals (one of the commonest forms of childhood phobia):

Wild beasts are as a rule employed by the dream work to represent passionate impulses of which the dreamer is afraid, whether they are his own or other people's . . . [19]

With the awakening of the repressed impulse, emotion becomes flesh.

What happens next? Freud's account would lead us to suggest three different sources for the construction of the phobic object. Firstly, a *splitting* of disavowed parts of the child's self: 'I do not hate daddy, I love daddy'; secondly, a *projection* of the repressed 'passionate impulses': 'I do not want to hurt daddy; daddy wants to hurt me'; thirdly, a *displacement* from the real object of fear: 'It is not daddy who wants to attack me, it is the horse, the dog, the tiger.' Freud continues:

We have not far to go from here to cases in which a dreaded father is represented by a beast of prey or a dog or a wild horse – a form of representation recalling totemism.[20]

In Freud's world, emotions are dangerous. It's as simple as that. It seems such an old-fashioned view that we are surprised when we realise it's true. I can love too much, be too greedy, plague myself with envy and hate. But it's all part of 'me'. In projecting the emotion, I am attempting to rid myself of bits of myself – dangerous bits that might be attacked if I kept them inside and recognised them as my own. A middle-aged woman refuses to accept that she has ever in her life wanted to cheat. The cheating part of her – the little girl on her third birthday playing pass-the-parcel, for instance – became so 'bad' and persecuted that it was expunged from her consciousness, and now exists independently. She cannot, even as a thought experiment, acknowledge it inside herself. 'It often happens', says Freud, 'that the dreamer separates off his neurosis, his "sick personality" from himself and depicts it as an independent person'.[21]

In waking life as in dreams, parts of the self can be separated off and appear to achieve independent existence away from us. Unfortunately, from that other place they can come back to haunt us. In an analysis of a restaurant phobia, the Kleinian psychoanalyst Hanna Segal suggests that unwanted aggressive, greedy, dirty and 'persecuted' parts of the self are thrown into the other people who may be encountered at the restaurant.[22] Colloquially, we would say that she is 'putting her shit into other people', and psychoanalysts take this in an almost literal sense. They do not take the metaphor literally because of some theoretical prejudice or personal predilection, but because of what patients say to them in analysis. Hanna Segal's patient remembered that as a child she loved the pink sugary pills she was given by her mother:

Till one day she was given one and to her horror found that inside they were full of a disgusting brown stuff. . . . She then remembered two bits of dreams from the following night: the first one had to do with a bunged up lavatory and in the second one she saw a child peeing into the soup.[23]

(Freud would probably point out that the onset of menstruation, regarded with horror in many cultures, may reactivate these earlier traumas and feelings of disgust.) However, the metaphor of 'dumping' onto other people does not capture the fundamental sense of disintegration or the mental pain that this particular patient was suffering from. She often felt depersonalised and unreal. She could form no relationship except on the basis of totally controlling her objects. Various hypochondriacal symptoms had led to numerous surgical interventions. Her phobias of crowds and food had led to severe anorexia. It was as if everywhere she went she was under attack from dangerous faecal bullets – of criticism, hatred, disdain, anger, rejection – being shot at her from other people. 'In phobically avoiding crowds she was avoiding the come-back of her projected disintegration.'[24]

Social panics and phobic objects

These mechanisms – splitting, projection, displacement – are instrumental in the construction of a phobic object both for the individual and for social groups. In *Totem and Taboo*, Freud describes the way in which malevolent demons are created in 'primitive' societies. Someone dies – perhaps an important chief or a big man of the tribe. There is emotional ambivalence in the survivors, leading to an internal conflict and splitting between the affectionate and hateful currents of feeling. The hostile part of their attitude (which is unconscious) is projected outwards onto the dead person, and the dead person is turned into a demon. As Freud puts it:

It is no longer true that they are rejoicing to be rid of the dead man; on the contrary, they are mourning for him; but strange to say, he has turned into a wicked demon ready to gloat over their misfortunes and eager to kill them.[25]

In scapegoating, too, a similar process occurs. The hatred and blame felt towards authority figures – the collective 'fathers' – may be disavowed and displaced onto others less powerful. There they can embody all the badness that has caused us misfortune, and can relieve us of the strain of our ambivalence. Thus, the deep-seated sense of national humiliation which traumatised Germany between the wars could be transformed, through ritual slaughter, into an ideology of national redemption. In blaming the Jews, we redeem the father; in forcing the Jews to take on our sins – the dirty, humiliated and greedy parts of ourselves – we redeem ourselves; and in eliminating the Jews, we cleanse the fatherland and become reconciled to our forgotten past.

It may be surprising to find that so much psychological energy can be taken up in maintaining the integrity of father figures. Historians have written of the panic that sweeps through a battlefield when the cry goes up that 'the king has lost his head', and we can see the effects in opinion polls when a population perceives weakness in political leaders. Nevertheless, how can a threat to the stability of the father – a largely symbolic construct after all – function in the same way as a failure in the function of the mother? If the breast is not there to feed you, your whole world is destroyed. No wonder it's scary. The mother is the environment in which you have your being. But if your father slips on a banana skin, it's not the end of the world, is it?

In that seminal work of cultural interrogation, *The Simpsons*, Marge Simpson goes to a psycho-analyst to cure her of a phobia of flying. It turns out that as a child Marge was told her father was a pilot – until one day she discovered that he was really a cabin steward. This was a devastating trauma to Marge. She had run onto the plane, eager to see daddy off, and there he was *in an apron* serving drinks. The subsequent phobia served to obliterate from her mind the scene and the humiliation – perhaps horror – it no doubt aroused. At this moment of disappointment, which happens to each of us in some form or other, there appears a kind of rent in the fabric of reality itself, a kind of anxious intimation that the world we know, or think we know, could fall apart; as if the collapse of the symbolic world is indeed equivalent to the collapse of the physical world. 'What am I even at the best but an infant sucking the milk Thou givest, and feeding upon Thee, the food that perisheth not', asserts St. Augustine, directly linking the symbolic world with the feeding relation.[26] Now imagine a crisis of faith.

The history of social panics shows how phobic objects can be created to deal with threats to the body politic. Periods of social transition or fragmentation are ideal conditions for the spewing forth of phobic objects. Witches cavorting with the Devil and bringing every misfortune into their communities; Jews killing innocent children and drinking their blood; Reds under the bed plotting to brainwash your neighbours: the language of disgust and horror is used for political ends to subjugate, disenfranchise, incarcerate and destroy.

Closer to our own time, single mothers, beggars, homosexuals and foreigners have all been used by governments to help maintain the status quo or provide a convenient scapegoat in times of crisis.

Stuart Hall and his colleagues described the social processes whereby the 'mugger' came to represent and crystallise threats to the social order in Britain in the early 1970s.[27] In tracing the subtle shifts of meaning which transformed the traditional white working-class crime of 'bag snatching' into the spectre of the black 'mugger', they described a complex tapestry of psychological and sociological threads. Fears of being violated, robbed and beaten were related to fears about the stability and intactness of the outside world, and were projected into the construction of the phobic object. Once the panic was localised, the mechanisms of the state apparatus – the police and legal system – could be mobilised to deal with it. Thus, it seemed perfectly appropriate to the general public that a black man should be sent to prison for twelve years for snatching someone's bag. One would hardly have realised from newspaper reports that, according to Home Office statistics at the time, young black men were many times more likely to be assaulted than other sections of the population. But the image of the rapacious black man was appropriate for the service it was required to perform. It spoke directly to unconscious hopes and fears which had been present for centuries:

The symbolism of the race-immigrant theme was resonant in its subliminal force, its capacity to set in motion the daemons which haunt the collective subconscious of a 'superior' race: it triggered off images of sex, rape, primitivism, violence and excrement.[28]

Inchoate fears could conveniently coalesce around the main templates of racism: black people as children, animals, monsters, faeces. Remember Gabrielle and her frightening 'black mummy'. Thus it was no accident that the black man became the 'phobogenic object'.[29] It was because he could encapsulate, contain and condense a panoply of fears and forbidden urges – sexualised phantasies of alien conquest, archaic fears of the evil demon, troubling intimations of the savage within. When one talks to a naïve racist (one whose hostility and aversion is not rationalised by a political conviction, but is a fearful visceral response), the (xeno)phobic quality of their reaction is evident. Immigrants bring disease, immorality, dirt, 'germs', bad smells, economic threat and an amorphous 'difference' that is hard to define but definitely bad.

In some cases, the phobogenic object becomes a cornerstone of the cultural system. In his compelling psychohistory of racism in the United States, Joel Kovel shows how economic forms are related to patterns of racism and the particular phobic meanings attached to racial groups.[30] He describes three forms or historical phases of racism: 'dominative', 'aversive' and 'meta-racism'. In the first case, characteristic of slave society, the rapacious savagery of the black man threatening the purity of the white woman is controlled through domination and violence. In the second case, the infectious dirt of the black person has to be controlled through avoidance. In the third case, characteristic of late capitalist democracies with their equal opportunities policies and the like, awareness of difference is avoided through denial that racism exists. In each case, the spectre of the black person threatens the cultural illusions and power structures of the status quo. Thus, other people or whole groups become the repositories of the unwelcome parts of the self, which can then function as phobic objects. The 'Untouchables' in India not only clean the toilets of the wealthy, but also signify the inherent attributes of dirt themselves in order to maintain supernatural legitimation of the caste system. In a million small ways, communities can regulate access to resources and relations between racial groups through phobic belief systems. When I was young, I was reliably informed that black people ate dog food. I rushed back home for my dinner and looked suspiciously at the plate.

They shoot horses, don't they?
Phobia as symbol

In the classic cases of phobia there is a remarkable degree of *condensation*. Condensation is an obvious characteristic of a phobia, yet it calls into question some of the psychological ideas we have been discussing so far. If the phobic person is projecting *fragmented* aspects of a disintegrated personality, why should these *coalesce* into a phobia?

Freud considered the issue in his infamous case of Little Hans.[31] Hans suffered from a fear of horses so intense that it left him at times unable to leave the house. I call the case 'infamous' because Freud treated it, and the observations upon which it was based, as a means to confirm the sexual theories he had elaborated in *Three Essays on the Theory of Sexuality*. In this earlier book, Freud asserted the existence of childhood sexuality; with Little Hans he gave the abstract theories a personality. 'I already knew the funny little fellow', says Freud, 'and with all his self-assurance he was yet so amiable that I had always been glad to

41

see him'.[32] Many students who first come across this case assume that Freud and the child's father (who is recording the observations) are putting words into Hans's mouth. We find it distasteful to contemplate the possibility that children may have sexual feelings or phantasies, and this produces a seemingly unbridgeable gulf between the psycho-analyst and the general public.

What both sides might agree is that a child's wishes are different from an adult's. When a child says 'I wish you were dead', we know that this is said with a child's understanding of what 'death' means, and does not contradict the tender feelings of love and the need for protection that the child also feels. When a child says 'I wish I could marry mummy', we know that this is said with the child's understanding of what 'marriage' entails, despite the childish passion with which the wish is articulated. Apart from the jokes among mothers at the school gates about the embarrassing comments little Johnny comes out with, it is rare that the child's passions and ideas are taken seriously. Children have sensual bodily experience and emotional relationships; they are curious about the riddles of existence – Where do I come from? What is the difference between boys and girls? – which they interpret according to their own theories and bodily feelings; they fall in love and experience jealousy; they have obscure urges and strange ideas hidden from their parents. In the collective denial of children's sexuality and phantasy life, we abandon them to solve these momentous problems on their own – and we fail to relieve the anxieties which lie at the heart of the child's sexual life.

That's how Freud thought about it. If the child wants to know where babies come from, he says, it's because he wants to know where this particular baby comes from – the one who may take away his mother's love and threaten his whole existence. If he wants to know the difference between boys and girls, it's because he feels a threat to the precarious identity that defines him as one or the other. In adolescence, the childhood fears may return. An adolescent boy may worry that he is growing breasts; a girl may be horrified by the hairs appearing on her body and for a fleeting moment imagine that she is turning into a man. The paedophilic representation of the child's sexuality as a sphere of pleasurable quasi-adult experience is a million miles away from the psychoanalytic understanding which sees sexuality as troubling to the child, and which places psychic pain at the centre of the human condition. In the latter case, the adult's role is to help the child through the inevitable anxieties, frustrations and disappointments that his or her sexual constitution and sensuous emotional experience will bring.

So Little Hans found himself in the Oedipal maelstrom. Nobody is surprised when we see the dramas played out nightly on our TV screens. Frank loves Pat but he's married to Peggy; Robbie loves the girl next door but he fears rejection; Sandra is torn between her child and her ex-lover. For children, too, the configuration of family life creates an inevitable psychodrama. Love and hate, jealousy and dependence, fear and yearning are all mixed up together. Ambivalence is at its height. It must seem that whichever way the child turns, there will be a danger. If he goes towards one parent, he may upset the other; if he detaches from one parent, that parent may not love him any more. If he feels angry, he fears retaliation; if he feels love, he conjures up the spectre of rejection. Parents who love and protect you may also attack you, abandon you, die, collapse, blow up, try to control you, and so on. Imagine this precarious state of affairs with all these possible dangers, real and imaginary, linked as they are to your own ambivalent feelings, intense urges and dependencies. This emotional cataclysm is the normal state of affairs for anyone growing up, and it is hardly surprising that childhood phobias during this period may be regarded as 'normal'.

For Little Hans, the phobic object, 'horse', was the repository of many fears. The horse may bite, it may fall down, it may die, it may run out of control, it may knock you down, and so on. One characteristic of the horse was particularly frightening: the fear that it would bite him. 'The idea of being devoured by the father is typical age-old childhood material', says Freud:

It has familiar parallels in mythology (e.g. the myth of Kronos) and in the animal kingdom. Yet in spite of this confirmation the idea is so strange to us that we can hardly credit its existence in a child.[33]

We are even less likely to credit the specific fear which, for Freud, provides the motive for the phobia in this case:

His fear that a horse would bite him can, without any forcing, be given the full sense of a fear that a horse would bite off his genitals, would castrate him.[34]

Freud first used the term 'castration complex' in a paper, 'On the sexual theories of children' (1908). It is one of the strange theories that children make up to explain the difference between boys and girls. What Freud saw in Hans was a little boy full of many fears, dominated by the huge shadow of castration anxiety. Castration anxiety was evoked as a result of his dangerous libidinal urges to have his mother to himself, and the observation that his mother and sister, long thought to be the same as him, were different in one crucial respect. Other characteristics of the horse pointed to the source of the castration threat. At one point, Hans became particularly fearful of what horses wear before their eyes, and by the black around their mouths. Freud suggested that these were visual references to his father's eyeglasses and moustache.[35]

Under investigation, then, Hans's phobic object or situation revealed itself as a complex amalgam of anxieties and impulses, and the result of numerous psychical mechanisms. There was the fear of being eaten (related to 'oral' conflicts and frequently depicted or alluded to in fairy tales), anxieties around 'pooh' and defecation (another 'weird idea' that nearly every parent has experienced with their young children), fear of losing his mother (separation anxiety), worries about his little sister Hanna and where she came from, and finally the dominant castration anxiety. Reviewing the case, Anna Freud remarks:

[F]ears and anxieties . . . are compressed by the

47

child into one encompassing symbol which represents the dangers left over from preoedipal phases as well as the dominant ones due to phallic–oedipal conflicts.[36]

Transformations

A man goes to analysis with a spider phobia – the spider might crawl into his mouth and kill him, or he may be pulled up into the web and eaten. In his 'real life' he feels trapped in a relationship of hate and dependency with his mother and the rest of his natal family. He remembers a childhood experience from the age of five.

He was playing under the kitchen table when his mother announced she had something new to show him. She pushed her face close to his and smiled, revealing for the first time her new dentures. He became terrified and screamed, for he was suddenly overwhelmed by a fear that she would devour him, immediately leading to a phantasy of his mother as a dangerous orally incorporating spider, which subsequently became the nucleus of the phobia.[37]

Leaving aside the specific meaning of the phobia, this story illustrates the cardinal theme of transformation of the benign into the malevolent, of seduction and betrayal, commonly found in children's fiction. Grandma turns into a wolf, the kindly old woman turns into a witch, the trusted teacher turns into a killer. The stories oscillate between fear and fascination, temptation and repulsion. On seeing the hideous and ghastly face of the Grand High Witch herself, the boy-hero of Roald Dahl's *The Witches* identifies the feeling precisely:

There are times when something is so frightful you become mesmerised by it and can't look away. I was like that now. I was transfixed. I was numbed. I was magnetised by the sheer horror of this woman's features.[38]

'Children who suffer from phobias', observed Anna Freud, 'not only flee from the object of their anxiety but are also fascinated and compulsively drawn toward it'.[39]

Adolescent horror films articulate some of the dangerous consequences of developing sexuality: hairs sprouting in unexpected places, putrid matter erupting on the skin, sexual 'pollutants' escaping from the body, swellings appearing as if from nowhere and, most significantly, intense emotional tangles with parents, teachers and peers. The films serve as a gory rite of passage, a defile to pass through from one state of being to the next. You probably know the kind of stories I have in mind: a group of students at a co-ed college visit the empty house on the hill for an illicit party, only to discover that the Dean of Faculty is a devil-worshipper ready to slice them up.

Younger children, too, worry about the integrity of their bodies and the protective nature of the world in which they find themselves. There is a frightening indeterminacy in the child's categor-isation of the world: the distinction between imagination and reality, between animate and inanimate, living and dead; trust in other people; ambivalence to parental figures; concerns about the vulnerability of the body. Feelings of psychological safety are evidently not as secure as we like to imagine. We carry around inside us, says Freud, an infantile morbid anxiety 'from which the majority of human beings have never become quite free'[40] – a precondition for the construction of phobias.

The horror, the horror: Edgar Allan Poe

A mother can turn into a witch, or a father can turn into a monster. But many phobias have an abstract quality that seems distinct from a relationship with living human beings, even if the relationships are distorted by phantasy. My own father, as a child and young man, suffered from a recurring nightmare: a nebulous shape was bearing down on him, two spherical objects like huge dumb-bells, threatening to crush him. Yet the real terror was reserved for the thought that if the two parts of the object came together, something terrible would happen. He had to keep the spheres separated and immobile, straining in the dream to keep them apart. Similarly, Freud's 'Wolf Man', as a child, dreamed of seven wolves sitting impassively in the tree outside his window. What terrified him was not the wolves, but their immobility. As Freud tells it, the passivity of the wolves was a reversal of the reality on which the dream was based. It represented the child's perception of his parents' love-making – the 'primal scene' interpreted by children as something violent and disturbing – and the passivity of the little boy, transfixed at the spectacle. A perception of violent agitation is erased in the wishful presentation of quiescence.

Thus, despite the fearful apprehension in the dream, it circumvents the anxiety which lies at its root. There is something uncanny about the primal scene, says Freud. The child does not understand what is going on, he does not know 'where to put himself'; he has obscure intimations and confused feelings, often of an aggressive nature; his world is turned upside down. He witnesses an act which speaks of a time before his own existence and threatens to create his rival, and in which his parents are monstrously transformed into a single beast. The perception squeezes him out of the family equation, yet draws him further in. Fascinated and repelled in equal measure, is it any wonder that apprehension of the primal scene may be something traumatic? If the dumb-bells come too close together, something dreadful will happen; but if they slip too far apart, you are left high and dry.

Considering the work of Edgar Allan Poe, the theme of betrayal is made horrifying and explicit. In so many of his works, a safe world suddenly becomes dangerous because somebody runs amok, or because impersonal forces of evil are mysteriously unleashed. The refined and considerate host becomes the evil torturer, refined only in the art of hideous death. You fall asleep and wake up in a coffin, buried alive with no one to hear your cries. The box which contained a work of art is revealed to contain a decaying body, and so on. Attachment theorists might argue that Poe's evident uncertainty, his lack of trust in the world and indeed his descent into alcoholism and gambling addiction all point to an early relationship marked by ambivalence and disruption. And indeed the facts of Poe's life support such a view.

Born in Boston on 19 January 1809, it seems that little Edgar had the great psychological boon of a happy mother. On the back of a miniature portrait of herself, Elizabeth Poe wrote: 'For my little son Edgar, who should ever love Boston, the place of his birth, and where his mother found her best, and most sympathetic friends.' This early idyll was not to last, however. By 1810, the family had moved to Norfolk, Virginia. His father, David Poe Jr., a travelling actor, had died or deserted the family and Elizabeth was left destitute. She died on 8 December 1811 in Richmond, Virginia, shortly before Edgar's second birthday. He was later adopted by the Allan family and sent to school in England when he was six. From the bare lineaments of this tragic story, one will hardly be surprised that the themes of betrayal, misplaced trust, helplessness and physical suffering are so evident in Poe's work. But there are other aspects of his writing that the vicissitudes of his early relationships cannot so easily explain. (The fact that Poe borrowed many of these themes from the numerous 'penny dreadfuls' and stories of the macabre that were fashionable at the time should not dissuade us from making psychological conjectures.)

Why should the themes of burial or immurement be so prominent in Poe's work? In 'The Cask of Amontillado', a man gets walled up alive in the cellar; in 'The Pit and the Pendulum', the walls of the cell begin to close in on the victim, threatening to crush him or push him into the dreaded pit; in 'The Black Cat', the cat that will not die is walled up with the dead wife; in 'The Murders in the Rue Morgue', one of the victims is stuffed up the chimney; while 'The Premature Burial' speaks for itself. A person suffering from the common phobia of travelling in lifts or being in confined spaces would sympathise with the horror that these depictions attempt to arouse. There is also a kind of unnameable horror that can only be hinted at. The prospect of being crushed by the walls of the dungeon, cut to pieces by the pendulum or eaten by rats is as nothing compared to the horrors of the pit which cannot be described:

I rushed to its deadly brink. I threw my straining vision below. The glare from the enkindled roof illumined its inmost recesses. Yet, for a wild moment, did my spirit refuse to comprehend the meaning of what I saw. At length it forced – it wrestled its way into my soul – it burned itself in upon my shuddering reason. O for a voice to speak! – oh, horror! – oh, any horror but this! With a shriek I rushed from the margin and buried my face in my hands – weeping bitterly.[41]

Perhaps little Edgar wept bitterly when the other momentous event of his first two years took place – the birth of his sister Rosalie when he was less than a year old. It seems inconceivable to many that such small children can intellectually register the events in their environment, or be affected by happenings which they cannot yet understand. Freud assumed – and modern research supports his hunch – that children know more and notice more than we give them credit for. What might the child scarcely old enough for thinking have made of the new arrival and the problem of where it came from? Or how might the experience have accrued meaning retrospectively as the child acquired new knowledge and emotional complexity?

Psychoanalysts have asserted that the contents of the mother's body is of supreme interest to the child. The phantasy of intra-uterine existence, the aggressive wish to rip out the contents of the body, and the body as the first object of philosophical inquiry, have been described by both Freud and Klein.[42] In another paper, Freud recounts a childhood recollection of Goethe's. Goethe is less than two years old, and throwing pots and pans out of the kitchen window, followed by the best china. Freud surmises that the memory serves as a screen for the desire of the young Goethe to throw out the baby that had recently arrived and usurped his favoured position in the home. In a flash, the great bedrock of his life had become the great betrayer. Freud tells of a similar experience in his own life.[43]

Imagine the turmoil of emotions as the child's stable world threatens to turn upside down. For Klein, the fear of retribution for the phantasied attacks on the mother may make the body 'a place of horrors'. If I want to attack your insides and scoop out the contents, you may want to do the same to me. In similar vein, Ricky Emanuel interprets the childhood fear of burglars and intruders.[44] In phantasy, the child invades the mother's body in order to damage or steal its contents; the impulse rebounds on the child as the phobic fear of intruders coming into the house to 'get' him. Such ideas might be reanimated during adolescence. We find the 'return of the repressed'[45] in the common themes of teenage horror films. 'What do you want?', asks the terrified victim trapped in her house. 'I want to see what your insides look like', replies the disembodied voice from the other end of the telephone.[46] The idea that such phantasies may exist at the deepest levels of our personalities seems abhorrent and unbelievable. It is when we see them enacted by normal people under stress that we wonder where this dark side of human nature comes from. The deranged high-school students carrying out the disembowellings in *Scream* would have been joined by their normal

The Birds

classmates had they found themselves together at the massacre of My Lai during the Vietnam War.[47]

But the mother's body as a 'place of horrors' is also our first home and our first place of safety. The subliminal evocation of intra-uterine existence can create the feeling of the 'uncanny', as Freud calls it, because we have experienced it before. Something from a previous existence is coming back to entice us, desired and feared as a place of dreadful pleasures and exquisite anguish.

If wombs are like tombs, it is possible to link the theme of betrayal in Poe's stories with the specific fear of being boxed in or walled up. It represents the horror and fascination of intra-uterine life. Or does it? At the risk of alienating even the most open-minded readers, I feel compelled to point out (as Freud did nearly a hundred years ago) that young children may imagine that babies are born from the anus. Understandably, they base their idea of birth on the template of their own bodily experiences. (The next time you're chatting with a three-year-old, just ask!) Sedimented in the unconscious, this strange idea can persist in the adult mind, and find subtle means of expression. The horror of the pit may be the horror of being trapped in the rectal canal, a place which, once valued, soon becomes the repository of everything disgusting and 'bad'.[48] So to explain this particular constellation of themes we have to take into account not only the history of attachment to the mother, but the phantasy life and unconscious desires of the small child as they reverberate in his developing mind. Perhaps, in the end, Poe's secure early attachment asserts itself: the victim about to fall into the pit is rescued in the nick of time; the poor soul who is prematurely buried lives to tell the tale; the descent into the maelstrom is ended by a miraculous escape; and in 'The Cask of Amontillado', the narrator, after all, is the one with the trowel.

A classification of phobias?

Psychoanalysts have explored a number of specific anxieties, and made anxiety itself a cornerstone of their theory and practice.[49] It would be convenient if the multiplicity of phobias could be classified in relation to a limited number of infantile situations which give rise to anxiety, but the complexity of the phobic object would suggest otherwise. The phobia does indeed *evoke* these situations – birth, helplessness, separation and abandonment, loss of love, primal scene, threats to bodily integrity (castration), death of self and others. It also *symbolises* some of our most frightening phantasies and sadistic urges. And it *represents* – stands in for – some of the people closest to us: mum and dad, brother, sister, and that shadowy critical figure which Freud calls 'the parental agency' and Klein 'the combined parent figure'. In 'evoking', 'symbolising' and 'representing', a developed phobia will have contributions from many sources. Nevertheless, in a particular case, one or other anxiety situation and phantasy content may predominate.

Freud himself confessed to a fear of trains, telephones and death, which might be classified as mildly 'phobic'. If we recall that journeys often involve separation from home, that death is frequently represented as a journey, and that disembodied voices may have something deathly about them, it would not take us long to find some unity in these phenomena around the common childhood anxiety of separation.

But how would we classify the bridge phobia? My friend crossing the bridge was, like Little Hans, fearful of a number of possibilities. The bridge itself, of course, which joins one side of the river to the other. The fear of falling, or being submerged, or drowning. Then there was the middle of the bridge, which seemed to be the point of greatest fearful anticipation. The edge of the bridge was terrifying, as was the gap between the two bridges. It is easy to find in all this a multitude of basic anxieties: separation (the middle of the bridge is furthest away from the safety of either side); the primal scene (if we assume that the bridge symbolically joins the two parental 'banks'); castration (the edge of the bridge as a cut, or the gap between the two bridges representing 'something that has been taken away'); and the primitive anxiety of falling into the 'void'.[50] Analytic investigation might enable us to find a dominant anxiety, but I suspect it is more likely we would find that anxieties from all phases of development can happily coexist. Moreover, a phobia is constructed from private meanings and unique experiences. Each element weaves itself into a story of everyday life that reveals long-forgotten passions and underlying anxiety. (Perhaps, as a little boy, my friend was frightened by dangerous thoughts and excitements when his parents left him alone with the babysitter each week while they went to play Bridge.) To be aware of the possible anxieties gives us a handle on phobic phenomena, but not a single key. There is no simple dictionary to tell us what they mean.

Confronting the monster: the function of phobias

Phobias function as part of the psychic economy of the subject. They are, in effect, bits of the mind which have been placed into the outside world. And they have been placed there for a reason – or at least there are consequences to them being so placed. Phobias have both intra-psychic and inter-personal functions. Intra-psychically:

- They are a vehicle for hateful and aggressive feelings.
- They help temporarily to circumvent the problem of ambivalence.
- They condense anxieties into a 'knowable' form and give some measure of control over them.
- They help stabilise phantasy activity and legitimate it.

One could even say that phobias have a progressive aspect as well; they offer the child and adult an image of the future – this is what you have to overcome in order to grow up.[51]

The central feature of *avoidance* in phobic phenomena hints at a connection to obsessional rituals. Freud saw the repetitive 'undoing' of obsessional rituals as a defence against 'temptation' – that is to say, the enactment of an unconscious phantasy – and against the impulses that lead to temptation. Thus, agoraphobia may be a defence against a dangerous exhibitionistic phantasy, claustrophobia may be a defence against a wish to go back to the womb, a fear of heights may be a defence against an uncontrollable impulse to jump, a terror of spiders may be keeping at bay the phantasy of ripping off their legs, and so on.

Anne-Marie Sandler has considered the role of phantasy in a more sophisticated way.[52] She posits two types of phobia: the classic 'extrusive' type, in which an internal danger is extruded onto an external object (through splitting, projection and displacement); and 'intrusive' phobias, in which the anxiety is aroused by the situation. In the first case, the fear performs an ongoing function in maintaining the internal equilibrium of the person; in the second case, the equilibrium is disturbed by the external reality. The phobic object or situation upsets the delicate psychic balance the child has achieved through phantasy activity. Children (and adults!) often develop phantasies in which there are attackers, robbers, wild animals, devouring monsters and the like. In imagination, the child triumphs over these figures or finds some other way to reassure himself that he is in control.[53] The phobic object is one which reinforces the frightening figures created in phantasy and creates a state of panic. It puts too great a demand on the person – they can no longer control the disturbing urges and impulses through phantasy. A child who was able to control threatening homosexual feelings through games and phantasies of foreign soldiers attacking him with bayonets, found his coping mechanisms broke down when he was required to go swimming. The phobic object or situation lines itself up with the (projected) hostile forces which are ranged against the child, and tips the balance. 'Intrusive' phobias are therefore not generally seen as part of the personality. The phobia only 'kicks in' during specific situations or when specific demands are made – for example, a fear of flying or swimming – while for the rest of the time the person seems free of any debilitating anxiety. Sandler further specifies the particular role of traumatic experiences in the causation of intrusive phobias:

[A]*n overwhelming frightening experience can act as an important organising agent for the child's subsequent fantasies.*[54]

In similar vein, the French psychoanalyst André Green has recently developed the concept of 'central phobic position' to describe the organisation of a central defensive core to the personality (defending against intense feelings or intimacy with others) caused by the impact of traumatic experiences.[55]

Childhood phobias occur typically during the Oedipal period, as in the case of Little Hans, at a time when the nascent (or, for Kleinians, not-so-nascent) superego begins to exert its influence. The free expression of libidinal and aggressive urges is no longer acceptable and, moreover, the child begins to fear the consequences of his emotional expression. In this scenario, the phobia may function as a kind of detached, surrogate superego controlling the child's chaotic and fragmented Oedipal impulses through threats of punishment. Just as a child's toy may function as an outlet for forbidden emotions and obscure urges, or its play be used to repeat traumatic events in its life, so the phobic object or situation both expresses the emotion and holds it in place. It joins the inner world with the outer, connecting the torrent of repressed urges and ideas with the 'parental agency'. The phobia is a kind of insurance: the parents don't turn into monsters; your ambivalent feelings don't tear you apart. The twin threats get drawn into the gravitational pull of the phobia. Paradoxically, it makes the real world safe again.

Finally, there is a conflict between what we might loosely call 'developmental forces' and forces which attempt to hold the subject back. Growing up not only offers opportunities and rewards, it also entails significant losses which the subject is not likely to contemplate without some degree of trepidation. The phobia can be seen as the result of an *impasse* between these competing tendencies, which may have the effect of blocking development. Just as a stomach-ache, headache or some other physical symptom may be used to justify a day off school, so the construction of a phobia may be a more permanent way to avoid the unwanted demands of reality. In other words, it keeps reality at bay and gives you a bit of space to grow up at your own pace.

In their interpersonal functions, phobias keep the parental figures 'good' (bad frightening wolf as opposed to good protective daddy), encourage idealisations, and also regulate 'distance' with parental figures. The child afraid of wild animals climbing through her bedroom window, or the possibility of spiders crawling into her mouth, will find herself in the parents' bed, a little girl safely protected from the traumatic awareness of Oedipal desires. In entering the parents' bed, however, the child is simultaneously experiencing these desires in their most intimate location while continuing to deny their existence. The phobia allows the child to maintain a dependent relationship, refusing the doubtful promises of Oedipal awakening and separation. In growing up, children are required to step off the Oedipal cliff into the unknown – but some stand petrified at the edge. And when you think about it, who can blame them? A phobia may be a child's way of keeping things in place while cognitive, emotional and libidinal developments realign themselves. If the child is unable to achieve separation, however, and early idealisations remain intact, the phobia may indicate a more serious split in the mind.[56]

Once again, Hitchcock's film *The Birds* offers a telling illustration. From one perspective, the film is a story of sexual awakening. It begins with (much older) brother Mitch buying a pair of lovebirds for Cathy's eleventh birthday. He wants them 'not too demonstrative' and 'not too aloof'. Just 'friendly'. The misnamed lovebirds are required to acknowledge sexuality and deny it at the same time, occupying a middle space of Oedipal safety. But to no avail. Faced with the impending eruption of sexual life, and the spectre of incestuous longings from the past, the violently repressed returns. Remarkable as it may seem (Annie is killed by the birds, while Melanie becomes catatonic), Cathy gets through the attacks unscathed. 'Can I bring the lovebirds?', she asks at the end, as the family walk precariously to the car through the carpet of squawking birds.

Treatment

Perhaps the relation to dependence and sexual

awakening is one reason why, above all other neuroses, phobias seem susceptible to a cure by 'love'. An agoraphobic woman may suddenly find herself cured after she enters a fulfilling sexual relationship, a man petrified of heights may show a remarkable ability at rock-climbing while in the throes of a first love affair, a hypnotist may get sensational results with suggestion. It is also why childhood phobias may gradually lose meaning, like a 'transitional object'.[57] A child who was terrified of spiders suddenly finds she can pick them up – 'at least the small ones' – and put them out of the house.

As for the treatment of phobias, psychoanalysts have questioned the efficacy of a behavioural approach which gradually habituates the person to the object of their fear. They argue that although results seem impressive at first sight, the fact that the underlying anxieties are not articulated and worked through means that they will simply attach themselves to some other object or another symptom altogether. I think this undervalues the direct approach. Freud advocated that in the analysis of a phobia there comes a time when you simply have to tell the patient to go out and face it. After the 'unfolding' of the phobia through the analytic process, uncovering the layers of phantasy and anxiety, the object of fear must be confronted and overcome, just as it must in the process of growing up.

One can hardly master a phobia if one waits till the patient lets the analysis influence him to give it up. He will never in that case bring into the analysis the material indispensable for a convincing resolution of the phobia.[58]

In the case of agoraphobia, for instance, one must encourage the patient 'to go into the street and to struggle with their anxiety while they make the attempt'.[59] If nothing else, it gives the analysis something 'real' to work with.

Freud doubted whether phobias could be classified as independent pathological processes, since phobic phenomena can be found in schizophrenia, obsessional neuroses and other conditions.

Charles Brenner is even more doubtful of the diagnostic value of the category:

If all phobias . . . were dynamically or genetically similar in many important ways, calling a symptom a phobia would be useful. In fact, however, the reverse is the case. The only thing all phobias have in common is the defensive use of avoidance. They share nothing else, either dynamically or genetically, which distinguishes them from any other class of symptoms.[60]

Similar symptoms can have different causes. Nevertheless, phobia – or 'anxiety hysteria' as it was originally called – has a right to be considered one of the 'founding symptomologies' of psycho-analysis, illuminating some of the essential aspects of its theory.

Notes

1. The 'objective correlative' is described by Eliot as 'a set of objects, a situation, a chain of events which shall be the formula of that *particular* emotion'. T.S. Eliot, 'Hamlet and his Problems' (1919), in Frank Kermode (ed.), *Selected Prose of T.S. Eliot*, London: Faber and Faber, 1975, p. 48.

2. Ernest Jones, 'The Psychopathology of Anxiety' (1929), in *Papers on Psychoanalysis*, London: Bailliere, Tindall and Cox, 1948, p. 294.

3. Ivan Ward (ed.), *The Psychology of Nursery Education*, London: Karnac Books for The Freud Museum, 1997.

4. Graham Music, *Affect and Emotion*, 'Ideas in Psychoanalysis' series, Cambridge: Icon Books, 2001, p. 38.

5. Sigmund Freud, 'Introductory lectures on psychoanalysis: Anxiety' (1917), in *Standard Edition of the Complete Psychological Works of Sigmund Freud*, vol. 16, London: Hogarth Press, 1953–73, p. 398.

6. Natasha Bondy and Sarah Cable (producers), *Phobias*, BBC1 production, July 2000.

7. Donald Spoto, *The dark side of genius: The life of Alfred Hitchcock*, Boston: Little, Brown, 1983, quoted in Almansi, 1992, p. 87 (see note 10).

8. N. Bondy and S. Cable, op. cit.

9. Evan Hunter, *The Birds*, directed by Alfred Hitchcock, 1963.

10. Renato Almansi, 'Alfred Hitchcock's disappearing women', in *International Review of Psychoanalysis*, vol. 19, part 1, 1992, pp. 81–90.

11. Anna Freud, 'Fears, anxieties and phobic phenomena', in *Psychoanalytic Study of the Child*, vol. 32, New Haven: Yale University Press, 1977, p. 88 (slightly amended).

12. Ibid.

13. Julia Segal, *Phantasy*, 'Ideas in Psychoanalysis' series, Cambridge: Icon Books, 2000.

14. S. Freud, 'The theme of the three caskets' (1913), in *Standard Edition*, vol. 12.

15. Donald Winnicott, *The Piggle: An account of the psychoanalytic treatment of a little girl*, Ishak Ramzy (ed.), London: Penguin Books, 1977, p. 6.

16. Ibid., p. 37.

17. Ibid., p. 36.

18. S. Freud, op. cit. (1917), p. 398.

19. S. Freud, *The Interpretation of Dreams* (1900), in *Standard Edition*, vol. 5, p. 410.

20. Ibid.

21. Ibid.

22. Hanna Segal, 'A note on schizoid mechanisms underlying phobia formation', in *International Journal of Psychoanalysis*, vol. 35, part 2, 1954, pp. 238–41.

23. Ibid., p. 239.

24. Ibid., p. 240.

25. S. Freud, *Totem and Taboo* (1913), in *Standard Edition*, vol. 13, p. 63.

26. Julia Kristeva, *In the Beginning was Love: Psychoanalysis and Faith*, trans. Arthur Goldhammer, New York: Columbia University Press, 1987, p. 24.

27. Stuart Hall, C. Critcher, T. Jefferson, J. Clark and B. Roberts, *Policing the Crisis*, London: Macmillan, 1978.

28. Ibid., p. 224.

29. Franz Fanon, *Black Skin, White Masks* (1952), trans. Charles Lam Markmann, London: Paladin, 1970.

30. Joel Kovel, *White Racism: A Psychohistory* (1965), London: Free Association Books, 1988.

31. S. Freud, 'Analysis of a phobia in a five year old boy' (1909), in *Standard Edition*, vol. 10, pp. 3–149.

32. Ibid., p. 41.

33. S. Freud, *Inhibitions, Symptoms and Anxiety* (1926), in *Standard Edition*, vol. 20, p. 105.

34. Ibid., p. 108.

35. S. Freud, op. cit. (1909), p. 41.

36. A. Freud, op. cit. (1977), pp. 87–8.

37. Ralph Little, 'The resolution of oral conflicts in a spider phobia', in *International Journal of Psychoanalysis*, vol. 49, parts 2–3, 1968, p. 492.

38. Roald Dahl, *The Witches*, London: Jonathan Cape, 1983, p. 70.

39. A. Freud, op. cit. (1977), p. 88.

40. S. Freud, 'The Uncanny' (1919a), in *Standard Edition*, vol. 17, p. 252.

41. Edgar Allan Poe, 'The Pit and the Pendulum' (1842), from the complete works of Edgar Allan Poe at Internet reference www.eserver.org/books/poe/.

42. S. Freud, 'On the sexual theories of children' (1908), in *Standard Edition*, vol. 9; Melanie Klein, 'The theory of intellectual inhibition' (1931), in *Love, Guilt and Reparation*, London: Delta, 1975.

43. S. Freud, *The Psychopathology of Everyday Life* (1901), in *Standard Edition*, vol. 6, p. 51.

44. Ricky Emanuel, *Anxiety*, 'Ideas in Psychoanalysis' series, Cambridge: Icon Books, 2000, pp. 36–7.

45. S. Freud, op. cit. (1919a), p. 249.

46. *Scream*, directed by Wes Craven, 1997.

47. Kevin Sim and Michael Bilton (producers), *Four Hours in My Lai*, Thames Television 'First Tuesday' series, date unknown, 1988.

48. Donald Meltzer, *The Claustrum: An investigation into claustrophobic phenomena*, Strathclyde: Clunie Press, 1992.

49. R. Emanuel, op. cit. (2000).

50. R. Emanuel, 'A-Void: An exploration of the nature and defences against nothingness', in *International Journal of Psychoanalysis*, forthcoming, 2001.

51. Donald Campbell, 'Discovering, explaining and confronting the monster', unpublished paper, 1995.

52. Anne-Marie Sandler, 'Comments on phobic mechanisms in childhood', in *Psychoanalytic Study of the Child*, vol. 44, New Haven: Yale University Press, 1989, p. 101.

53. Ibid., p. 109.

54. Ibid., p. 107.

55. André Green, 'The central phobic position: a new formulation of the free association method', in *International Journal of Psychoanalysis*, vol. 81, part 3, 2000, pp. 429–51. See also Robert Gillman, 'The Oedipal organization of shame: the analysis of a phobia', in *Psychoanalytic Study of the Child*, vol. 45, New Haven: Yale University Press, 1990, pp. 357–76.

56. M. Masud R. Kahn, 'Role of phobic and counter-phobic mechanisms and separation anxiety in schizoid character formation', in *International Journal of Psychoanalysis*, vol. 47, parts 2–3, 1966, pp. 306–13.

57. D. Winnicott, 'Transitional objects and transitional phenomena', in *International Journal of Psychoanalysis*, vol. 34, part 2, 1953, pp. 89–97.

58. S. Freud, 'Lines of Advance in Psychoanalytic Therapy' (1919b), in *Standard Edition*, vol. 17, pp. 165–6.

59. Ibid., p. 166.

60. Charles Brenner, quoted in Allan Compton, 'The psychoanalytic view of phobias, Part IV: General theory of phobias and anxiety', in *Psychoanalytic Quarterly*, vol. 61, part 4, 1992, pp. 426–46. (Parts I–III of this article can be found in the same volume.)

Dedication

To my friends and family (without whom this book could not have been written)!